BOOKS BY ANSELM HOLLO

POETRY

And It Is a Song
Faces & Forms
The Coherences
Tumbleweed
Maya
Alembic
Sensation 27
Black Book
Some Worlds
Lingering Tangos
Sojourner Microcosms
Heavy Jars
With Ruth in Mind
Finite Continued
No Complaints
Pick Up the House
Space Baltic
Outlying Districts
Near Miss Haiku
Blue Ceiling
High Beam
West Is Left on the Map
Survival Dancing

SELECTED TRANSLATIONS

POETRY

Some Poems by Paul Klee
Red Cats
William Carlos Williams: *Paterson* (in German, with Josephine Clare)
Allen Ginsberg: *Kaddisch und andere Gedichte* (with J. C.)
Gregory Corso: *Gasoline und andere Gedichte* (with J. C.)
Paavo Haavikko: *Selected Poems*
Pentti Saarikoski: *Selected Poems*
Pentti Saarikoski: *Trilogy*
The Poems of Hipponax

PROSE

Jean Genet: *Querelle*
Franz Innerhofer: *Beautiful Days*
Olof Lagercrantz: *Strindberg*
Peter Stephan Jungk: *Werfel*
Lennart Hagerfors: *The Whales in Lake Tanganyika*
Jaan Kross: *The Czar's Madman*
Jaan Kross: *Professor Martens' Departure*
Rosa Liksom: *One Night Stands*

PLAYS & SCREENPLAYS

Bertolt Brecht: *Jungle of Cities*
Georg Büchner: *Woyzeck*
François Truffaut: *Small Change*
Louis Malle: *Au Revoir Les Enfants*

CORVUS

POEMS BY ANSELM HOLLO

COFFEE HOUSE PRESS :: MINNEAPOLIS

Cover illustration by Jane Dalrymple-Hollo and the author.
Back cover photograph by Jane Dalrymple-Hollo.

Some of these works, several in earlier versions, have appeared in *Active in Airtime*, *Anatomy: Raw*, *Basura*, *Bombay Gin*, *The Bombing of Iraq*, *Books from Finland*, *The Cafe Review*, *Dark Ages Clasp the Daisy Root*, *1844 Pine Street*, *Exquisite Corpse*, *Fell Swoop*, *Gas*, *Hanging Loose*, *The International Review*, *Lingo*, *Make Room for Dada*, *MEANTIMES in Dis Place*, *New American Writing*, *The New Censorship*, *Notus*, *Poets Say Goodbye to the Twentieth Century*, *Proliferation*, *Prosodia*, *PsaLm 151*, *The Poet's Notebook* (W.W. Norton), *Puerto del Sol*, *Rain City Review*, *Scarlet*, *Sniper Logic*, *The Shambhala Sun*, *Talisman*, *Tule Review*, *The World*, and in the chapbooks *Blue Ceiling* (Tansy Press), *High Beam* (Pyramid Atlantic), *West Is Left on the Map* (Dead Metaphor Press, with drawings by Jane Dalrymple-Hollo), and *Survival Dancing* (Rodent Press). The author is grateful to the editors, publishers, printers, and distributors of these publications.

Coffee House Press is supported, in part, by a grant provided by the Minnesota State Arts Board, through an appropriation by the Minnesota State Legislature, and by a grant from the National Endowment for the Arts, a federal agency. Additional support has been provided by the Lila Wallace-Reader's Digest Fund; The McKnight Foundation; Lannan Foundation; Target Stores, Dayton's, and Mervyn's by the Dayton Hudson Foundation; General Mills Foundation; St. Paul Companies; Honeywell Foundation; Star Tribune/Cowles Media Company; Beverly J. and John A. Rollwagen Fund, Prudential Foundation; and The Andrew W. Mellon Foundation.

Coffee House Press books are available to the trade through our primary distributor, Consortium Book Sales & Distribution, 1045 Westgate Drive, Saint Paul, MN 55114. For personal orders, catalogs or other information, write to: Coffee House Press
27 North Fourth Street, Suite 400, Minneapolis, Mn 55401

Library of Congress CIP Data
Hollo, Anselm.
Corvus : poems / by Anselm Hollo.
p. cm.
ISBN 1-56689-039-X (pbk. : alk. paper)
I. Title.
PR6015.0415C58 1995 95-31691
821' .914—dc20 CIP

10 9 8 7 6 5 4 3 2 1

Table of Contents

For Ye Raven's Mistris:
"Evermore!"

Author's Note

Why "Corvus"?

In the first Middle Ages (our present era being the second), Latinizations of names of non-Latin origin were relatively common. Had I lived then (and especially if I had been born in Hungary instead of Finland), my last name could have been *Corvus* or *Corvinus*: in Hungarian, the raven is *hollo*. And *Hollo* was the name my paternal Finnish great-grandfather adopted after a family dispute whose causes are lost in the murk of time.

The word has no lexical meaning in Finnish; it was simply the traditional name of a piece of land he owned. Finnish and Hungarian belong to the Finno-Ugric/Ural-Altaic family of languages and share a relatively small proto-vocabulary; but the modern Finnish for raven is *korppi*, borrowed from Latin *corvus* via Swedish *korpen*. Both *raven* and *corvus* derive from the Indo-European root *ker*, "to cry out." (Joseph T. Shipley, *The Origins of English Words*, Baltimore, 1984)

I have always admired that uncompromisingly elegant bird, in all its mythical and legendary manifestations. I even like its *ker*, more appropriate to the poetry of this century than the trills of the nightingale.

My favorites are Odin's two ravens, Huginn and Muninn: after flying all over the world, they return to sit on his shoulders and (no doubt hoarsely) whisper the news into his ears.

As ever, the news is both sad and glad.

1991

i.m. Irina Hollo (1921-1991)

morning sun
strikes me pow! in the face
I turn and see

first of all
a small black wall of fur

hear it purr
then see beyond it *you*—

were that five-mile-diameter asteroid
to hit
right now
this very moment
in the age of post-fatalist
neo-feudalism
it would be no big deal
sub specie aeternitatis
"in eternity's sight"

but I'd sure hate to miss
what continuance
of these momentitos of bliss
the gods may still grant us

fire stairs dark
                    against crimson sky
tall brick walls across the way

moonlit trees & snow a herd of deer
                    asleep in the yard

two frames of the window
movie

          only we
          have seen

Lost a tooth had it fixed
took winter's first tumble on icy front step
received the news of my sister's death
all the same day

So you "took and died"
"*otti ja kuoli*"

Here we say
"up and died"

Where to go in the mind
for language to say
así es la vida
You liked that phrase "such is life"

We do much prefer the suchness of life
to the suchness of death

Older by thirteen years
last one to know me
as a child

Used to think of you there
"among all her things"   Now
we stand here
among all your things

Babble two minutes
in father's tongue
then sit down all pale
(my task at the rites)

At the rites we think of the old days when belief
made words reach the dead

a resonance
gone

OK Sis
now of no fixed address in the Kingdom of Dis
Miz Ubi Sunt

your departure sent us out of our patch in the sun
to fly with the ravens
back to the granite the lilac the moss
my "horse" tree with that bend
country and city of childhood's end

> "one of the pines has a bend in it
> three feet off the ground
>
> "the horse's back
> about two feet
> the neck then stretching straight up
> to the sightless head of it
>
> "where it becomes so fine
> there's no way of telling what goes on there"
>
> 1971

looked up at the window of your secret abode
turned
to see what you saw:
boats
  gulls
    skerries
      the Sea
        to the Western Lands

In your old cities
Helsinki Stockholm Londinium
you walk to the corner store
walk
on paving stones
smaller feet of yours walked on
past stone walls that sheltered a smaller body

Look up at the sky
out to sea
far seems as far as ever
but there is less time to get there

more time, now, in the stone
you have given your time to the stone
cities of stone built by your species fellows
Mr. and Mrs. Brainbrawn
who live and die faster than stone

Think these thoughts
go to the sacred places
the corner stores
light, warm, full of kind
perishable things
for you and you
one foot in front of the other
over the stones

aye . . . past
this bubble of assumed person
glassy shapes of the dead *en la noche* drift
beyond glad or sad
fugitives
from all personal referents

and as I step into the King Sooper's
in Boulder, Colorado
I almost trip
over the man in front of me
who's kneeling and bowing to Mecca
while his two ladies wait by the shopping cart

the cricket you hear
is not the cricket you heard
when, and when, and when

sat in front of the window

naked

she combed his hair

and he

that instant

achieved

complete

perfect

immortality

Among the more obvious conjectures an analytical reading of this text fragment yields are (a) that the author lived in a dwelling with windows, or at least was familiar with the "window" concept, (b) that he or she was also familiar with the notions of "clothed" and "naked" (= "un-clothed"), (c) that people of the period indulged in (sometimes mutual) grooming, possibly with implements described as "combs."

The second half of the fragment, moving, as it does, into abstraction, presents some difficulty in the realm of what we, for lack of a more precise term, may call "tone": are we to understand the statement literally (in which case the fragment has to originate in a theogony, a work describing the origins of gods—"immortals"), or metaphorically, as a hyperbolic expression of the emotion experienced by the male protagonist of the fragment, at the epiphanal moment described?

When we consider, furthermore, that there was a period around the mid-twentieth century in which some authors of "metaphysical" texts employed the phrase "instant perfect (or "complete") enlightenment" to describe a state possibly achieved by students of certain systems of thought management, we may even perceive a degree of irony in the substitution of the term "immortality" for the expected term "enlightenment"—an irony which seems to undercut anticipation (or likelihood) of either state described by those terms. If the fragment dates from the period in question, we may assume that the author was a bit of a skeptic in regard to said systems and their vocabulary.

"the poem machine should not mean machine
but be machine"
—Darrell Gray, after Archibald MacLeish

the trouble with

the being born machine is the subsequent trouble
of the being alive machine

and finally
the one of the dying machine
nevertheless there are times
of which it can be said

that we were
                              are and will be
flying
               without benefit of any machine

and when it happens we know it

Some Greeks

Family legend has it that my paternal grandfather, a master cabinetmaker in rural Finland, once became so enthused by the classics that he tried (in vain) to persuade his womenfolk to wear Greek garb while going about their domestic chores—in the summer, presumably, since the climate would have made this rather impractical during the rest of the year. His eldest son, my father, translated Plato, and my father's closest friend was the poet who first performed the *Iliad* and *Odyssey* in Finnish.

When I was ten, my sister lent me her copy of Schwab's three-volume *Tales of Classical Antiquity*, in an original German edition with interesting, faintly comical, engravings of scantily clad "ancient" goddesses and heroines and their consorts and adversaries. I found those tales a lot livelier than the monotheistic Biblical ones I was obliged to study in religion class (no separation of church and state in that time and place). If I had to choose among gangs of deities, I would still feel more at home with the old Greek one than with any other, including the Norse and Finno-Ugric which are presumably "mine" by "ethnic" heritage.

Later, when I read Plato, Sartre, Whitehead, and Wittgenstein, it often seemed to me that the pre-Socratics were still the most serviceable philosophers I had come across. (Permit me to recommend Guy Davenport's and Stanley Lombardo's sharp and scholarly translations of Herakleitos, Empedocles and Parmenides, published by Donald M. Allen, the great unsung Merlin of U.S. poetry, in the mid-seventies.)

Some time ago, I was struck once again by the similar freshness and timeless timeliness of so many of the texts we refer to as *The Greek Anthology*—circa 4,500 poems and fragments of poems written, sung, and spoken in the course of almost two millennia. Kenneth Rexroth's *Poems from the Greek Anthology* may have sparked my first love affair with those works.

My present selection was inspired by another volume, *Jalkapolku* ("The Footpath") by the Finnish poet Pentti Saarikoski (1937–1983). "The Footpath" is Pentti's personal anthology-from-the-Anthology, and his approach, "to let the poems themselves decide how they want to be said *now*," makes him my main collaborator, although I have also consulted other versions by worthy but (to my mind) mostly less inspired poet-translators as well as the hardy perennial Loeb Classical Library.

Like Christopher Logue, who in *War Music* and *Kings* has dared and brilliantly mastered the task of making Homer come alive in late-twentieth-century English, I have no classical Greek. "I was not . . . making a translation in the accepted sense of the word," says Logue, "but what I hoped would turn out to be a poem in English." He calls *War Music* "an *account* of Books 16 to 19 of Homer's *Iliad*." I shall be content if this handful of Greeks, as well as my translation of *The Poems of Hipponax of Ephesus*, are found to be acceptable accounts (or "overdrafts"—Basil Bunting's term) of their originals.

where the 3 roads meet
I was surprised to see   the great bronze of Hermes

knocked over, flat on the ground:
people used to worship it here . . .

now the invincible guardian
lay flat on the ground

but later that night he appeared by my bed
grinned down at me, said:

"you have to go with the times . . .
that much I learned
when I was a god"

Palladas

the poet Eutykhides has died—
watch out, you dwellers of the underworld!
here comes Eutykhides with his Odes!
it was his last wish
to be buried
with twenty-five trunks of *text*!

now
Death's grip is truly total—
how can there be
"eternal rest"

when *he* gets to rave on
even in Hades?

Lucilius

someone spoke of your death
Herakleitos and I thought
tears
        remembered
our walks in the morning rain

you've long been dust
my Halikarnassian friend
but your "NIGHTINGALES"

live on: omnivorous
as he is
            the death-god
he will not touch them.

(POSTSCRIPT)

2,240 years later, I have to admit
I was wrong about the death-god:
he did eat your NIGHTINGALES
he must've liked them better than my EPIGRAMS

Callimachus (& Anselmus)

When Diaphon
was crucified
he saw beside him a man
on a *bigger* cross—
and died
of envy

Lucilius

the only one sober
in a bunch of drunks
he looked high as a kite

Lucian

I love everything about you
except for that indiscriminate eye
that deigns to notice—
well, jerks

Rufinus

O Thaleia how I yearned
        to have you stay the night—

now, naked, you lie on my bed
        and I feel rather limp

come on you sluggard! get up!

this may be your last
        window of opportunity!

Rufinus

in the dead of night
in pouring rain
I flee from my husband

soaked   I arrive at your door

well   here we are

Philodemos

each morning we're born again
of yesterday nothing remains
what's left   began today—
so, old man,
don't be proud of your years:
what's past isn't yours

Palladas

Hello, Earth?
Yes?
You have Kharidas down there?
You mean Kharidas,
son of Arimmas? Yes, he's here.
May I speak to him?
Yes. Here he is.
Kharidas!
What's it like down there?
It's dark.
What about resurrection?
No such thing.
And the infernal majesties?
They don't exist.
Oh, that's terrible . . .
Well, you can say one thing for this place:
the rents are real low.

Callimachus

Blue Ceiling

raccoon sees Cat go in and out Small Door

          the mental beanie rotor turns

the mammal ever-blissful when it eats

                    "ah, Earthlings—"

one might of course say there haven't been any further poets
since Pierre Reverdy

sentence understood only if read at right tempo, said Ludwig
          then he wrote it down
and now we're reading it:
          "avoid" "arguments" "with" "the" "furniture"

the magus is dead long live the magus
                    semper bogus
(by now we should all know what people really like)

then tried to wipe a smudge of light off the table
with all the fussiness of an old, er, void
          it's all a struggle
cuttin' time
                so mighty fine
you won't be able to verify any of this

life's just a dream remember
    poetry just an interruption
of the great conversation
        farewell notes from those gone
weave through the composition

        a father walks in an old apartment
    talks: "never admit you're rich or asleep"

as you enter the recording studio
you notice you don't have anything to record

    skepsis is contemplation

        may you be forever strange
    may neither spring nor ashes faze your dailiness

what's ragged should be left ragged

    "we want the guided tour!"
slow thoughts down
    notice tone and sensation

bus bounces into pothole
    with delicacy and precision

when you met him he was a man
        now he is a postage stamp

you can't open the window this is Dallas

                "they took my billiard table!"
        Mary Queen of Scots complained in 1576

                mice fall from the sky

mind suffers body suffers language suffers
thinking urge greater than any other
bugs in throat in the dead of night

but what's past is yours in the vectors of joy

                in a café named after Beatles song
        person plays homemade instrument
combining tuba violin and gong

the unconsciouses
        slow as hazardous waste
roll through the night

Americans still know how
          they know how
to manufacture a good working handkerchief

          "It's real surreal!" said little Laura

fantasies magicks
          all come from the child
                    to work its will on the giants
then it grows up to be a giant itself and then
          there is still
the whole goddamn universe

          "It's never enough, is it?"

the poet you hardly knew
          looks dear and old like you
not like you but old like you
                    and dear to you
          on the cover of his "Kings"
not like thin dark peacoated figure
          glimpsed from a cab this spring
                    strode past Brompton Oratory
          large take-out coffee in hand
his double from half a lifetime ago

and the closetful of magical toys
                        shrank
          to old shoebox of objects broken and shoddy
now having neither
          you have both

slowly they walk across the sunny parking lot

they
          are your friends

". . . mad as Cassandra
who was as sane as the lot of them"
          in the footsteps of Jesus Tom and Jerry
perfect their running-in-air trick
          proceed
                    at speed
off edge of cliff
perform their midair miracles
then plummet backpedal hover and soar
over America
not to answer the question she asks

                    but to return
                    the question
                    to her
                    to change it
                    and return it
                    to her who asks
                    shall be the whole of the teaching

green rhubarb leaf-dragon
dormant under snow
beneath red studio wall
"merely a matter of belief"

in December
or *any* time and (whaddayaknow)
so is the snow
the red the green

the wall the house the art
what keeps it all
from flying apart
if not the love that moves
the sun and other stars

    and around midnight
    raccoon lady
        stops
    just short of the doorway, peeks in—

    trundles back out
        tells her companion

    "No good, he's still there
    in his chair
    reading *Harper's*"

West Is Left on the Map

?

trace my life on the map
a new geographical treatise
every day

check the table of contents
let's see
where will I be tomorrow

—Mihail Cosma

Worstward Ho

—Samuel Beckett

wee terrible human race
soon to go down   or else into space

let it go let it bleed
into stellar fuzz   the light of another sun

whatever it ever was
fights among capos

a puff of dust where the lampshade bloom'd

Marlene forever young

like Marx or Helen's ankles
at the gates of dusk

or a recital
of Etruscan tunes   what a treat

"poems in 2091
objects of monkish interest"
sez Vidal
Gore, not Peire

like poor but civilized urban existence
another thing of the past

Petrus Kalm (1716–1779), a native of Finland, went west & later wrote in his "Travels in North America":

"once this old white man went to the woods with one of the savages
& they came upon a
speckled red snake
the old man reached for a stick but the savage begged him
in the name of all that was sacred
not to hurt this snake
saying it was
one of his gods
so the old man picked up a sturdy branch & killed the snake
& told the savage:
'when you said to me
that this creature
was your god
you left me no choice but to kill it'"

& if that old man had not been so old
he would have killed that savage too
no doubt

yes   that's what's wrong with them

n o

d o u b t

watch out

for the wailing Fundees
& *their* "god"

their god grows out of the muzzle of a gun

Odyss   on the old plate
looked so comfortable in his body   old enough
to fit a few words together

bare twigs
                    cracks in the sky
long lines short lines no lines

let us sit down & enjoy a really empty experience

                              write what? to a tree?

"dear chords of night: one is not rhymes
but civil fur   come to bliss late"

this creature called god
               left one no ma

boat sails into sun

west
          is left on the map

an endless warble of dreams

Was there a time when thou, too, wert an optimist,
Falling about in fits of pseudo-mystical glee?
Sho' nuff—when Goddess Utopia roared in mine head
& I refused to be of time & place . . . Well, I still do,
Still wince at epithets that smack of Church or Nation
& would prefer to be, not just *El Hombre*, but *El Animal*
Invisible—one of those invisible beasties of the Lapps . . .
A follower of Lingo Rapture: she is never opaque,
Turn as she may—Mother Discourse, ever transparent
Even when terrorized by vagaries of head & heart
Sad, dignified as the winds on the moon
—minimalist intensity! Ah, well, the fire went west
& whims and winds took hat & head. Without
A head, no cigarette. Without a heart, big trouble.

remember Bear's Head who saw
between midnight & dawn *1833*
ten thousand meteors
cascade across the heavens
from the constellation we call The Lion

remember Bear's Head who saw
a comet in the sky
between midnight & dawn *1858*

remember Bear's Head who that same winter
in dreamtime
between midnight & dawn
saw canyon waters rise
& flood the land
& wash away his people *Arapaho*
saw
when the flood subsided
only the white men remain

remember him
who saw these things between midnight & dawn
in this place *Boulder*
on this planet *Earth*

all hail
to Mother Mail

3:30 p.m. the view is
Flatirons above trees &
neighbors across the street
in the window a rear end
of squirrel for half a nervous second
of its life (my life, your life) & that
does of course include
the front end too, my front end
is waiting for the mail
Great Mother Mistress MAIL
be praised: you bring the best, you bring
the worst, but "Lots of mail! I feel pretty
good!" said Ted in a poem, "I open
a beautiful letter from you. When
we are both dead, that letter will be
Part Two of this poem." Give us
our mail fix today & every day
oh I can remember when it came
twice a day, a dear old man
bending to pick it up off the mat
after it shot
through the slot
in our apartment door
in Helsinki, Finland
in the early years
of the millennium

"so what's the diff
between a hopeful sort who believes he'll go to 'Heaven'
& a hopeful sort who believes his descendants
will colonize the universe?"

asked Tattered Old Bird
minor warlock
invisible when at the top of his form

& the tribes unfurl the old demon banners:
oh let the dark ages begin again   so we can join
our dimwit ancestors in gore & glory

most of the populace blank
resigned to the neo-feudal

Geronimo stern: "YOU FOOLS!"

God is a speckled snake

cat turns mouse into mouse dust

"have a nice day"
said Tattered Old Bird
"have a nice dog have a whole bunch of fine gods dogs & days
in view of the indignities that await us
that doesn't seem too much to wish for
on the way to the old *pulvis et umbra*   *il faut s'amuser, non*?"

& the shades they are a-massing
at the gates of ghostly Troy

trying not to be
pissed off because
the truck won't start
(too cold)

I pick up a book
peed upon
by long-dead cat
in distant other life

& see the stain's
still there—
of the cat
not a whiff

but find the poems
of the late urban ironists
still pungent & deeply
amusing

so let the truck rust
the book
take me back
to streets once walked
nights
talked
dusk to dawn
in the Aeolian cities—

"borne
deposited
produced
eroded
by the wind"

think "son"
night's sleep gone

"we know you're in there"
locked inside
a crowded hippocampus world

of drums & demons
distance   absence

haunted years
of wish & rage

in mislaid brain
& slaughtered time

so the ghoul weeps
he the ghoul
weeps so
for his son

come out please come out
arise
take up thy bed   rejoin
whatever we might be
outside this maze

walking through a geometry
in a gold & green light
reading a sculptor's notes:

to create latent motion
you set up something
one would expect to move
but it doesn't
it remains
in the same place & position
& it keeps doing that

as eye & mind
repeat the event
that does not occur
again & again
you might call it
a raging balance

space
is mostly
light

what's tactile reaches out
grabs the 8 corners
of the room   (Ivan Liljander)

in Heaven which was the darkest corner
of the tavern right next to Diogenes
we hung out over cappuccinos
& munched on tasty raw veggies

I told The Old Dog
people on earth had finally managed
to kick the nasty expensive habit
of raising & eating cows

Diog' said Pythagoras
would have liked to hear that
personally he said
being the first citizen of the world
I've never been one to proscribe anyone's habits

then we leaned back to listen to Gerry
Mulligan play "Waltzing Matilda"

& as delighted as I surely was
to hang out with my favorite Cynic
I was homesick for Earth
& wished you were there with us

(not worried at all
you wouldn't know how to deal
with The Old Dog
who wasn't really a misanthrope
merely defined
anthropos
very strictly)

then opened my eyes
to the light & your eyebrows
& the golden light of your eyes

for him her face
goes out of focus
before his does for her

so that when she's
in focus for him
quite adorably he

seems sadly distant
to her but they refuse
to be terrorized

by that or any
other contradiction

though but a weave of dust and shade
caught in the chandelle of our days

who writing shovels grief's doubloons
I can say this: hello! dear woman I name Dream

dear called Because
with you, a thousand years would not be long enough

Not a Form at All But a State of Mind

"The sonnet . . . is not a form at all but a state of mind. It is the . . . dialogue upon which much writing is founded: a statement then a rejoinder of a sort, perhaps a reply, perhaps a variant of the original—but a comeback of one sort or another."

—William Carlos Williams

I

after reading the tiresome review
from the school of tedious outpourings
the man of letters is writing some letters
"would we all be happier in the factory?"

embittered romantics one and all
"we are but older children, dear,
who fret to find our bedtime near"
in the land of invisible warfare

vast cheering in the distance
hand me my spear   my little secret book
of matches   and footnote fame! oh
give me footnote fame

"but that's how my mind works" he said
desperately singing in harm's way

II

poppy or charms can make us sleep as well
joyful ants nest in the roof of my tree
full of courage and shrewd decisions
given to   marked by melancholy

my most rash eyes want out into the light
in that fierce place where love holds court
and there encamps   spreading his banner
where even wingless soar on balmy winds

in too-thin garments   see with no eyes
shout without a tongue
in a forest alive with whispers
soon-dead deer dash past

strange unrelenting world
I have woven my heart into this net of branches

III

wipe the screen   screw wigs on tight
as we grow older our nervous systems decelerate
many thoughts return marked insufficient
postage   "you know how to walk into a bar"

or any box in the postindustrial ruins
most of what we say is in quotes
we like wilderness in nachur
but not in our fellow citizens

amor armor amok   emery   immure
yes yes that does describe your arbitrary foci
on a warm wet noon   think "thought experiment"
or murmur "vagaries of the heart"

a comeback of one sort or another
dream of big live teddy bear that "wants" "you"

IV

it is well known that Mary Magdalene came to Provençe
to live after the crucifixion
but less known that at Maximilien near Marseilles
the tip of her nose used to be on view

no more than that   because she had been cremated
but the tip of her nose remained imperishable
because there   the christ had kissed her
& who is going to pay   any attention to anything

when we aren't here anymore   "& what was it *like*
that *world* of yours?"   so much depends
on Fire Engine Number 5   myth is the practice of memory
dit Joanne Kyger

Johannes Kelpius first american composer
founded a commune called "the woman in the wilderness"

V

the lecturer's heart stepped into the void
the mind slows down the mind speeds up before
it stops   contemplating what's never isolate
"landing a B-52 in a desk drawer"

the man said   spoke of his dying
I believe this is the future site of my plaque
life so short this piece of paper so small
alphabet ends   universe begins

still trudges along in its big shoes
not afraid to include   what seems dull & quotidian
replicas of your thoughts
win free admission to the shores of forgetfulness

at the edge of some divine comedy
the prompter whispers leftover lines

VI

vast cheering in the distance
embittered romantics one and all
on a warm wet noon   think "thought experiment"
or any box in the postindustrial ruins

alphabet ends   universe begins
at the edge of some divine comedy
"the sound like a thousand falling bird beaks
in the brown harpsichord of the grass"

in the last light of evening
and fear has lien upon the heart of me
in a forest alive with whispers
given to   marked by melancholy

a commune called "the woman in the wilderness"
so much depends on Fire Engine Number 5

VII

"days when the giant won't fall for the ruse
days when no kindly mammals speak to us with human voices"
i dunno man it's tough   & it's never been anything but
many were here but they left again

yet surprised once again
in awkward bliss and bashful ecstasy
let us forgo all pain of crags
here in this pleasant valley of diphthongs

come babe   pass me the delicious
cold cucumber salad
as the axe of the sun descends
we wane away among the peonies

& we have absolutely no complaints
of hours such as these

VIII

"would we all be happier in the factory?"
in the land of invisible warfare
many thoughts return marked insufficient
most of what we say is in quotes

win free admission to the shores of forgetfulness
& we have absolutely no complaints
let us forgo all pain of crags
for a special additional performance

of such as love and whom love tortures
like the eyeglasses of the less fortunate
in that fierce place where love holds court
joyful ants nest in the roof of my tree

myth is the practice of memory
"the pneumatic drill destroys my cities"

IX

underground trees   slow darkness
and fear has lien upon the heart of me
magpie steals silver spoon   it is gone forever
like the eyeglasses of the less fortunate

in a terrifying gray light from the future
the carnival continues   a place where a sad horde
of such as love and whom love tortures
point to the moon and break it

"in the year 1327   at the opening of the first hour
on the sixth of April   I entered the labyrinth"
yesterday's clowns return
for a special additional performance

in the last light of evening
today I think about all those radio waves

X

hand me my spear   my little secret book
desperately singing in harm's way
yes yes that does describe your arbitrary foci
dream of big live teddy bear that "wants" "you"

life so short this piece of paper so small
replicas of your thoughts
& it's never been anything but hours such as these
as we grow older our nervous systems decelerate

in a terrifying gray light from the future
I entered the labyrinth
full of courage and shrewd decisions
in too-thin garments with no eyes

at Maximilien near Marseilles
"at night the streets are tidal like the sea"

XI

"we are but older children, dear"
of matches   and footnote fame! oh
on a warm wet noon screw wigs on tight
not afraid to include its big shoes

when the cyclops won't fall for the ruse
as the axe of the sun descends
the prompter whispers leftover lines
I think about all those radio waves

where even the wingless soar on balmy winds
shout without a tongue   strange unrelenting world
after the crucifixion   "& what was it *like*   that *world*"
oh footnote fame   the man of letters

"you know how to walk into a bar"
in the year 1327   at the opening of the first hour

XII

"but that's how our minds work" they said
"who fret to find our bedtime near"
in any box in the postindustrial ruins
wipe the screen   amor armor amok   emery   immure

"landing a B-52 in a desk drawer"
the lecturer's heart stepped into the void
where no kindly mammals speak to us
come babe   pass me the delicious diphthongs

the carnival continues   yesterday's clowns return
my most rash eyes want out into the light
I have woven my heart into this net of branches
spreading its banner of attention

underground trees   slow darkness
murmur "vagaries of the heart"

SMALL DOOR AT FAR END

I

"time for your take, you assholes"
concern yourselves with what will sell
dead senses rule over a dead mind
the old fall silent and expire

their art consisted merely of the trick
that organizes production for *profit*
rather than for *use* (to find the right size of shoe)
because of you lady I am this way   a stubborn murmur

naked   extremely complex   gigantic
a barrage of labyrinthine winks
present culture not inevitable but offspring
of a particular form   & how *do* you spell "Rousseau"

ask Diogenes   ask Terry Eagleton
ask any intelligent slave

II

always but not unpleasantly torn between
transparent intelligence saying itself
"my poetry is mainly just talk"
economy elegance switching into surprises

& the total Sargasso Sea of signifiers
"they do my *research* for me"
releasing language from rules & structures
demonstrating its restrictions and hierarchies

Eisenstein cantos   Tzara words out of a grab bag
mental & linguistic exercise
think about each word and why it is where it is
moon splashes borrowed light on the wall

across the street of distant galaxies
slowly turning their tails to point to the first letter

III

"le plus souvent il s'agit de tristesse"
it is mostly a question of sadness   the trick's to remember
that *that* is absolutely *no* excuse to be boring
or humorless   or too conveniently absent

not to metamorphose
into moon splashes borrowed light on the wall of sound
keep in mind all of us have lived
are and will be living "interesting times"

of unprecedented   we're beginning to understand
insanely excessive   numbers of human beings on the planet
and therefore   at least quantitatively speaking
unprecedented magnitudes of loss injustice oppression

and weltschmerz   "sorrow or sadness
over the present or future woes of the world"

IV

"curiosity—advice to the young—*curiosity*" EP
to Vanni Ronsisvalle in 1968
slowly turning their tails to point to the first letter
"it is important to keep old hat in secret closet"

concerns charmingly optimistic
bohemie-anarcho-individualistic
oh give me Elysian   give me Eleusinian
city parks where Egil Skallagrimsson

enjoys a nude picnic with Emily Dickinson
satyrs converse with cyborgs
dinosaurs roam across the street
of distant anarchic galaxies

but they have devastated our great cities   & the poets
left there must wear the Star of the Marginal

LINES FROM TED: AN ARS POETICA

"Plagiarism—Good! Communism—Bad!

You can't fool anyone
You can't fool anyone that knows anything

But anything that you can use, you should use it"

—Ted Berrigan at Naropa, July '82

I

Ho Chi Minh wrote poetry
Richard Nixon didn't have any interest in any art at all
And Richard Nixon had all the chips
Ho Chi Minh didn't have any
seemingly
But of course as it turned out he had them all
It was not because he was a poet and Richard Nixon wasn't
But perhaps because he was a bit more aware of . . . Nature . . . I
/ mean
The President of the United States
as long as he's in office
Doesn't drive his own car   Ho Chi Minh didn't have that
/ problem
He couldn't find cars very often
When he could he probably found a driver
But usually he was running down some trail looking for a cave
Because enormous airplanes were overhead trying to bomb him
It kept him alert

II

It's true that Form does follow Content
Except that that sentence is gibberish
Those nouns and that verb don't go together
That's like saying the egg follows the picture frame
Which no doubt it does   But not in any way
That we are entirely sure of   except when we say so
We could say form is always and only an extension of content
But then we are liable to sound very peculiar
Only certain people are able to get away with
Saying things like that
Form and Content   That's like saying
If you cut off someone's head and destroy their form
Then you fuck up their content
Well that's true that's true
But you don't *know* much more by saying that   I'll tell you

III

I sometimes wonder
I sometimes think about how many poets
For example those poets in the universities with suitcoats on
Some of whose works I like very much nevertheless
How many of them broke their own hearts
Fighting against their own natural tempo and pace
in order to try to write
What was supposedly the right tempo and pace
For English-American literature?
You have to make your work at your own pace
It is made of words
One word after another
Some people do it in phrases
Others are beautiful writers of sentences
& some are beautiful writers
of one word at a time

IV

All this business of keeping score
& knowing who's good and who isn't   Fuck it, man
All those that are no good   Why are you thinking about them?
Even if they're famous?   Don't worry
If they're really no good they'll disappear after a while
And even if they don't   So what?
I mean, why are you going to be mad at them?
Because they're taking money out of your pocket?
That's not why you do it
If you want to get some money in your pocket   Get some!
If you have a talent for it you'll get some
If you don't   You got a problem
But just solve it some other way   Ask Allen for some
Only not this week

V

There is a standard above which you want your poems to be
If you do five hundred above that standard
And they're all very similar
That might not be having done such a great thing
But what I think happens when a poem works is
That it rises into the air of its own powers
And in doing so it has formed a circle
And it becomes something like the sun or a star
Or a planet
                    Or whatever
I like the idea of it being up in the air
            To have no idea is a good idea
            If it helps you to make a poem
I have to go now
I have to go and think about this for a thousand years

VI

The arts are something given to human beings to do
They improve your senses
It is necessary to do more than earn your daily bread
Shelter & food & ability to get the medicine
For your children when they have a cold
It's necessary to be more of a person than that
As Kenneth Koch said once
                                        it would be a very difficult life
To be the only Surrealist at the University of Minnesota
            You don't need company to be a Surrealist
            You need company to be alive
We could not be poets if we didn't use words
                        Perhaps there are animal poems too
You can be fat lazy poet & still be a pretty good poet at forty
Survival
              is the hardest test for a poet

VII

You are faster than your consciousness
Just like everyone knows a lot more than they're able to say
"How do I know what I mean until I see what I say?"
Say "ooga-booga" and see if you can think of something to say
Next
          It is a story
But you often leave out all of the plot
                    because it's poetry it's song
It's song pierced by intelligence with all that feeling in there
          You *have to* write a lot of garbage
          you may even find a way to include some of the garbage
          in your best poems
And make those poems be more like places that *include* garbage
You can come and sit up here and be a great guy
But you can't make a living

VIII

When you sleep under a tree and have a good night's sleep
You don't say "My new house is a lot better than my old house"
Except if you want to be poetic
I mean it's not a house you know it's a tree
Houses have mice and rats and things like that in them
And trees have crickets under them   For one thing
Because everybody knows something
          But as Frank O'Hara once said
          "I'm assuming everything is all right and difficult"
& Robert Lowell said
"I learned everything from William Carlos Williams"
And Allen said "Good God! *What did you learn*?"
& I said to Bob Creeley "Bob, how was your day?"
& he said "Well . . . I was reading Shelley"

IX

Once in my life I batted against a pitcher
Who played in the majors
He hit me right in the leg & I went down like I'd been shot
& I had a bruise on my leg this big for about a month
& he wasn't even really good
When I saw that ball coming it was coming so damn fast
I was just looking at it
I saw it was going to hit me right in the leg
I braced to hit his fastball
& it came and hit me in the leg & it hurt horribly
I fell down and said   I didn't say anything
I wasn't Pete Rose
But then   It's time
It's all about time

X

The Real Problems are
Like whether or not you should go
To bed with a certain person
Because they have beautiful handwriting
You know as in Lady Murasaki's book
Whom I once had an adventure with
And by that I mean exactly that
                                        an adventure
No poet worth their salt has less
Than a hundred books in their house
Unless they just sold some to pay the rent
But they'll still buy some more next week
The poet Kenneth Patchen was a poet
Of extravagance   The imagination of extravagance
We don't have many of those now

XI

You can become a Black Mountain poet
If you wish   All you have to do
Is find out what a Black Mountain poet is
& you'll never find out by asking a Black Mountain poet
All music is music   That's a good sentence
It doesn't have any meaning
"Take these brains from my pillow"
What's funny? What's so funny?
It isn't funny   Literature is not funny
Poetry is not funny   It's not funny to be a poet
It's not funny to be alive
Though it is pretty funny but
You think it's funny
You should find out how much I'm getting paid

XII

Hip? Try to talk your way out of whatever you did wrong
When you're talking to the policeman
            the farthest you can reach is your *hip* pocket
But the policeman is *not* the guy
            you're supposed to reach in your *hip* pocket for
But somebody up higher
I mean it's difficult to be hip
It's difficult not to be, too
If you learn everything about writing
From some supposed terrible boring Academic poet
That doesn't matter   It's you
It's what you want and what you write
Or if you want to write like some horrifying Beatnik
It still doesn't matter   it's what you write

xiii

If there's a little room up there
A waiting room that you can wait around in
For five hundred years
You can check from time to time to see
What they're saying back there on Earth
As to whether you did it or not
"He did it"
But as for one's self
One can't use the word *did*
ever   See?
Because you're not dead
So it's just like you did that   & you did this
but did you do it?
But even with Shakespeare
There'll be fifty years when they'll be saying "This guy
You don't have to read this guy   Read *that* guy"

xiv

The poet whose works you love
Who's changed your life
& given it shape   & become a Great Moral Source
Of Support in your life
May just be a prick with a bad character
Don't let that worry you
They just have bad days all the time
If you're vulnerable to never wanting to read their works again
when you find that out
Then never go any closer to them than this
Because it's the works that are the truth
Every person has a right
Poet or not
to be judged by their best
The only credit poets get is for being poets
Then putting their words together   & coming up with poems

PTERODACTYLS

I *"Publication date first of October"*

from Zlatko's Serbo-Croat   via fast translatese French
into "my" English   his journal scrolled up Macintosh screen
these summer months   hoping he lives to see it
I think of him often   & of his city's Utopia of *convivencia*

"while you are not safe I am not safe"   Ginsberg in *Howl*
when Sarajevo falls   all of us multi-ethnic bastards
who pray in *all* the temples   like all kinds of food
& minds & bodies every color shape & size

we better start digging our foxholes in the fourth dimension
& while we dig let us chant We Piss on the Serb Nation State
We Piss on the Croat Nation State   we piss and shit
on all your godforsaken states

murderous money-making machines for greedy sleazeballs
lording it over slaves who failed to teach their masters

II

tread the fine line between farce and pathos
torque your thoughts in the mental (not metal) bookshelf
hermeto-(not herpeto)-linguistic
shrine to Mr. Hun Tun
professionally known as "The Gourd of Chaos"
walk up & down   walk off & on   sleep off & on
far off   far off in the Gobi Desert   what can you say
you can say   & you won't be far off
"I have my love to keep me warm." & I can say
"'Yes,' he said. 'Yes, of course.'"
then you can sleep it off   & it may well be
what all these pronouns are saying
is merely the tremulous gibberish of just another other
talking to the page with an old child's fingers

III

i.m. Ernest Hemingway

trying to impress felines
strange hairless ape with mad eyes
too tired to explore postmodernism
"a rare   *luckier* kind of guy"
checks in at Perfect Cloud Hotel in Laphroaig
it is 9:15 a.m.   a Fundador brandy, please
yes, he would like to join the Lotophagoi
(old Ez   he wrote it down)
so let's just *decant* it in here
time to wind up the world no more substantial
than a good tune   oh fairer than the evening air
marked by slender delight   what we feel
is what we believe we feel   see say and be loved
despite much dull material to-be-forgiven

IV

for Tomaz Salamun

a long sentence: "son, write longer lines"
a green Pegasus, dancers, yaks
sing, masters of the universal pibroch
sing, balalaika, in the teeth of adversity

but don't you think it's time for Comrade Blank
to retire, with the understanding: *no more poems!*
sing, you "few buckets of water tied up
in a complicated sort of figleaf" (EP)

great solar, you stir, wake each exile man
marmoset, mormon, clits and toes
& tiger faces in the fire, Colonel North
got to the shredder in time to deconstruct history a bit

dig, with man, up feeling
here, with Doctor Who, in Deseret

VILLONELLES

I

cloud with delicate
cottonwool monkey face   drifting by
tape   drifting by   the magnetic heads
& into the spaces   between other heads

magnetic   electric   from here to everywhere
possibly back   & on out
some recall a musical theme
by having the score's image appear before them

then reading it   it is conceivable
that what we call remembering in a human being
consists of her seeing herself (mind's eye)
looking up things in a book

thus what she reads in that book
is what she remembers   Wittgenstein Zettel 653

II

someone blown clean down the block
shrieking with merriment shock
plant on table trembling
many-talk-in-head my name

duration between each death & birth
the seeds of karma   dynamite
little paws folded big paws folded
stagecoach takes corner   plenty of dust

master babe mandragora
shrieks when torn out   shrieks when rammed back
appearing reappearing
uttering language in extracurricular states

the idiot wars of the young   the idiot wars of the old
tape drifting   Zettel drifting

III

among the boulders in the huge scarred seam
a dwarfish person of the Queen's retinue
trying to speak whereof one cannot
said nothing but waited
playing with the hilt of his dagger
they usually keep a distance above ground
he thought
                    above the surface of things
as one who had never seen a mirror might wonder
in what depths of it lay the face she saw
heat waves raced & shimmered round the basin's rim
we'll find a way she whispered never fear but kiss me
notwithstanding the abruptness of this introduction
set like a stone he took a deep breath

IV

the people came out staring & pointing
their whispers rising like surf all about her
her features blurred & swayed before him
gloomy & wild is the air of this place

spring you get for free she thought & mostly it doesn't
turn out too well but then life's strength lies embedded
in a fresh coarse evenness
dense like any good production of Mnemosyne

slowness & sun have stayed with me
in calm & gentle absurdity she thought
frequent narrative climaxes   moments
of great suspense   & moments out to lunch

may be saved by one's ability to characterize
one's mythic role by comic ineptitude

V

again the owl's hoot pierced the night
wolves came up to the doorsteps of the rich
eager to miss
                    none of their syllables
"did you enter this house for loot or lore?"
ghosts do not eat
                         she rose from where she sat
ready to pounce
                        believe nothing I say
                        the town is hot
                        he takes to the road
a thousand *merci*s
                         I've been absent a lifetime
I spread my thanks at your feet

death's dark sack gaped
but you heard the snows
amid the jangling harps of hell
that gibber at each dream of peace

VI

toward morning we begin to feel insubstantial
our knees cease to shake we wrap ourselves in our cloaks
& proceed to the grove of oaks
twisted & windblown   clutching the stony planet

with roots of authority   purple & scarlet
retract periscope   trees & language in & out of a hat
slowly the ice of the unformed universe dissolves
in the world to come   everything like it was

in the world that was   yet everything quite changed
narratives   disjunctive (yet) associative as dreams
poems   sonorous   replete with handsome words
while lacking all "sense" & "connection"

the future world is sensible chaos   chaos squared
or raised to the power of infinity

REVIEWING THE TAPE

i.m. Piero Heliczer

I

calling 1959 calling 1959   what does he know
a red piano   a fragmentary tusk
he sees men & women preparing themselves
for the long journey across the room

he is in love with the world
it's got a face like a horse
her hair is 365 poems   a tent   & into it
that tune   it's 1790! oops   he stops   goes back

sleeping is any handful earth
waking returns the toothbrush clack to the beaker
"her anger has caused me great pain"
can't tell which she he is talking about

brown photo   legend
man's reliance on fossil fuels but a short episode

II

no junipers no shouldn't think so no
he wrote   somewhere inside
so slow   a broken nose   repeating itself
into this hole in the ground

no connectives or interval music
it was hot in the dream hole
above the brick town with its captive dogs
the first time you saw it   acres of watery sand

ah to be funny in bed in writing
to be in our bodies
maybe it was just his old difficulty
of remaining in the upright position

of the higher primates
their glimmering moments of loving

III

the instruction manual lay soaking in the bilge
I'm yours I'm all yours   but the signals were garbled
one who looked tall rode away
didn't have much to say

narrative   pomp & pleasure
time in shore zones

ahead of the water they came
wrapped round a stick of incense
he'll sleep a long time
the day your son comes home

a flute & a spine in the grass
too dark   a raving madman
persistent cigarette burns on his hand & arm
november 1967   a hundred farmers plow to lucid murmurs

IV

to disappear   on the floor
in the other room   closing the book
"I'll be back in a minute"   flowers out there

over them reigned a red personage
in autumn some sponges   "i am moving
a fraction to the weaker taking"

this deep a breath is ardent
ultimate consummation of long ethereal affair
sit listening to the gods
approach her   their cries

it is peaceful peaceful
the people go crazy
the manager of this cinema
wears a big floppy heart ha ha

v

branching like any body
but here   have some wine
& exhale heaven   snug against her skin
kiss her   ill with love

"him now"   in his sleep he walks past it again
to one who lives there
in the rented satellite
with Officer No Quarter

enters another plane
of the new world   or drives the big white car
through savage people & frozen gases

still taping   his thoughts ran much upon this
wrote the works ever known as
the features of gods

vi

on the horse's back & into a hall
then son   simply expressing   in his own way
that I was wrong   6–9:00 a.m.
through customs in Hong Kong

all the way to her navel
a single large crystal
thinks of Don Giovanni
with no interference from tree-cutting crane

smileful girl   they used to spend maybe an hour
in glamorous roles
in a little while it won't exist

red mists of rage
plate glass breaks   snow streels in thoughts
across a green roof

VII

there is a light on   prudent alchemist
laughs like Leo the sun
crocodile curbs dangerous onslaught
Iaia of Kyzikos   her pagan will to realize

life in the sky   she saw
a tapir do the tango
prance from his mother's house
back where the night begins

in a seven-foot urn
I move about   the beetle wakes up
temporarily in charge of the 1920s

the surface extends all the way out to the core
wherever there is a hole distributed in space
cave equals room equals window

High Beam

BORN TODAY

for Jane

is to be one to the one
closest to you
who shares the air
& other elements
right there   next to you

two bodies wrapped in darkness
among millions of other bodies
wrapped in darkness & smoke
war bloodshed & chaos
        voices rising out of the dirt

one to the one   without whom one
wouldn't be one
        who saves one when lost
in regions of the past
raging at bygone constellations
                pursued by a swarm of angst gnats
        who saves one by her sight & sound & touch
to notice
          that gravity's strong on this planet
notice
        there's a half-ton of apples in that tree
notice   cricket jumping on cedar branch
         feline humor   magpie elegance
in sum
        this world
born not so long ago
with maybe not that far to go
                still roaming
        the contradictory corridors
of a universe or two

wind turns pages   then shuts book
he looks up   she looks up from piano keys

                hold that frame

HOKA HEY

Into the Valley of Death
rode the six hundred
shouting
"DIG IT!"

—Ted Berrigan & Anselm Hollo
at the National Poetry Festival,
Allendale, Michigan, 1971

PROPOSAL

for war memorial to end
all war memorials:

plain granite slab
David Jones style lettering
text by Ted Berrigan:

THE WAR GOES ON
AND WAR IS SHIT

SWING HIGH SWING WOE

sleep
        unperturbed
"no
self"
moment
of blind spot
reached
at last
(margaritas . . . payday . . .)
then up
with a start
in love's arms
to Terra's hard rain
her drums of dread

yet even at zero
once glorious with friends

green light
                    on a lizard that caught you watching

Δ

let mute edge of night knot a rat

wick wither

                    gaze roll out to the dark

like trembling bats

                              their petals still coiffed

CHICAGO

up and down he went
in the pink elevator
                                        in the pink hotel

where pink (and, well, some rather ashen)
Elders
        dwelled

went up & down
as all their lives before
                        but now
in these
        "controlled circumstances"

they had, in fact, *become*
"controlled substances"

this occurred to him
as he stepped out of the pink elevator
to meet young friends
                                        under the grand chandelier
where they sat chatting
with some Elders
                                in clown masks & wild paper wigs

A TOWN DEDICATED TO THE PURSUIT OF FITNESS & INNER PEACE

says the headline   so that's where we are
that's why they're building
fifty new houses
right next door

now the telephone wants to tell me about a deal
on cleaning our carpets & upholstered things

I tell it "we don't have any"
then replace it quite gently
in what I believe is called its cradle

yes among those alive today
we're truly fortunate
to be living these charmingly specialized lives
in "a town
dedicated to the pursuit of fitness & inner peace"
unlike the majority of the planet's towns
which remain dedicated
to plain old pursuit of food
& staying alive   a few moments longer

yes fortunate   if a bit haunted by Kafka's Fear
of waking up in less delightful state

but that comes & goes
just like the battles of light & darkness

old hats bursting out of their secret closets
to be stuffed back in   to reappear thirty years later
empty as ever (no brains) but plenty of clout

very fit for his age
the Senator
enjoys
his inner peace

LIT. GROUP HISTORY

It was their intention
to gain recognition
as a group. Later,
they would remain friends

but wait to be "cut out of the herd"
by some young
perceptive
Lit. Crit. hand.

BLUE MARCH '91

brute metal glee
momently done careening about that Gulf

wind blows dustballs and spiders
out of the walls

to sort
black socks
in the dark
is your task

the Species invented Time
and probably Space

its function to be their recorder
until the End

young beauty
picks up spider
re-locates it
in flowerpot

SCHILLER'S ROTTING APPLES

think thoughts think
desire: wanting that thinks & feels

ah the ukuleles of yesteryear
praise the Lord & pass the graham crackers

watch the last dukes of reaction
jet round the empire the vampires they are
while listening to Chet

    Chet the great
    cool cat

    cat fell out the window
    cat went splat

shadow moves up & down tree

        life is of course utterly

Q & A

wake language
delve into mulch
anyone there?

similar life
out in the dark
and proud of it

SARDANAPALIAN SURF

frozen
H_2O
falls from the sky

Sun Ra has set
Dizzy spun out & away
into the universe

"what means
this *universe*?"

flowers of sound
turn & return

at indeterminate
intervals
of continual change

these be the means
by which it
flowers

O KEATS WHERE IS THY STING

"thorn stuck in paw
bullet lodged in leg
bee buzzing in ear"

ah, *nell' mezzo cammin*
to steal one's script back
re-write it for better & worse—

once again it is time
for our jitterbug lesson

NOTE FOUND ON MEDITATOR

war bonnets horsemen a waving forest of lances

                    a lovely sight

          if you don't care for what they're attacking

it's John Wayne they're attacking OK no problem

                    beauty

knows no ideologically correct routines

                    beauty knows nothing at all

that's why she asks all these questions

THE FIRST JAZZ AGE
(OR, OH NO NOT ANOTHER E. M. FORSTER MOVIE)

dancing's
pacific
non-utilitarian
formerly 'sacred'
use of Legs

motoring's
expression of universal
human
Angst

Dancing + Motoring = the Twenties

or so one imagines

---

as life gets shorter
art does too

(the twentieth century: one third of it over
by the time I got here)

hung out with the infallible long enough
now give me some fallible ones

watch out! here comes a giant of discourse

to deflate
the peripatetic time bomb

"lazy pig lazy pig lazy pig"

FROM THE HELLIAD

"bulldog faces of ex-generals"

processed responses

a fast re-wind

to where once again
the shod & housed

wipe out the shoeless

(at least "try their damnedest")

Δ

no war is holy

war

is made by the holier-than-thou

it enthuses the pointless

Deep-fry those petrolized cormorants

serve them to Presidents

G. Bush & S. Hussein

Winter 1991

THREE FOR ED SANDERS

1. SOTHEBY'S 2094

Cat. Item 4711. Holograph letter from Edward Sanders, dated 12-10-93, with copies of two poems, *Amazing Grace* circular, and magisterial missive to Poetry Project Newsletter, complete with hand-addressed envelope, in plastic bag issued by United States Post Office Denver CO 80266-9701 with pre-printed (sans-serif) apology for severe mutilation of all the above items contained therein, caused, by the looks of it, by robot canine interference with postal sorting process. Tattered papyrus effect does not interfere with delightful contents, *inter alia*, Mr. Sanders's poignant "Bard Plank" diagram. Fascinating late 20th century item. $150,000.00.

2. VERSES FOR AMAZING GRACE

amazing face you are my joy
at dawn at noon at night
though life be frail the gods but boys
who kill us for their sport
I praise each day dawns on our bed
to light your human form
here next to mine when night has fled
and we are here once more
together in this raging world
this human universe
together in this human world
this raging universe

& Jane's quatrain

the stars will adorn the cold clear nights
the sun will bring the dawn
the wind will sing the seas will dance
long after we are gone

3. TRULY, WE LIVE IN SINISTER TIMES

"... *in finsteren Zeiten*" —Bertolt Brecht

Amazing face, you are my joy—at dawn, at noon, at night ... But there is also the matter of outrage: a *human* emotion, brought on by *human* actions. At bedtime we read this book about the *gods*—great stuff, much of it quite horrendous—but then the *gods* decide to give us so much to do that by the time we get to bed we're way too tired to go on with it, or much anything else, for that matter. I wonder if *they* think we shouldn't find out too much about *them*, now that *they* are so busy fomenting human wars again?

That's all very nice, even whimsical. (Nothing wrong with whimsy, unfashionable as it may be.) But the truth is that we live in an age in which, once again, clan and religion rule by feud; in which zombies make and sell killing machines & zombies buy: "I blow out your brains ha-ha you're dead I feel so alive!" Brains ... too big, too small? Nervous systems, too complicated, too crude?

In a besieged city where all the trees have been cut for fuel, more people are murdered daily for wanting to share that city with Others, as they have done for centuries—by other Others who say

Now you must die
or go live with Your Kind
because we
can live only with Ours

—while we, champions of "multi-culturalism" over here, go about yes indeed our *business*, saying oh it's all too confusing, we'll just have to let them sort it out somehow ... Truly, whom gods wish to destroy, they first strike with blindness. Men, made stupid, made implacable by men, made stupid made implacable ... ad infinitum, it seems.

OK boss off to the supermercado
hairless apes with mad eyes
civilians at large   grazing in aisles
I'm in a panic—what shall I do

why I'll just blow out your brains
ha-ha you're dead I feel so alive
look at these rare
historic photographs

depicting life in a city
where every tree's been cut for fuel

WRONG CHANNEL

old Ez
more prophetic than he knew
re: world's return to feudal

"Purgatorio to Earth
Purgatorio to Earth—
this old geezer was right after all
future planet
needs good tyrants"

QUESTIONS

Josef Hellström & Emiliano Zapata
met? in Mexico, 1911? hung out
with Ambrose Bierce?

    our heads
    the "heaven"
    where they engage in lively debate

FAMILY OF CAVE BEARS

she used to wind that watch once a day
before she moved into the wall

drew her last breath of rage
against the injustice of dying

so he wrote it down
one early December blizzard night

she's dead
and so are all her habits

IN THE OLD BIOGRAPH

WATCHING THE TAPE

what if one recorded every
waking possibly even sleeping
moment of one's life   up to say thirty-five
then spent one's remaining years
watching the tape?

STORMY WEATHER

night ride down a wide avenue
black   a-glitter with rain: *der Kurfürstendamm*
a walk past the *Reichskanzlei* and its stone-faced sentries
in 1939   age: five

THREE FIGURES FOR EDWARD GOREY

night falls
        on Niagara Falls
& on the bridge
        stand mother sister
and the informant
        (sole survivor)

MY SISTER LIKED THE POSTCARD OF SNOW

          White and the Seven Dwarfs
she kept it for many years

it rises
          out of the memory banks
in all its stupid glory

                    & so
          does Dinky the toy dog
light as a bird-bone

THEY

are here
in the auras
of the furniture

INHABITED EYES

falcon-eyed Montcorbier
gone complicated after much dying

sang about April
in nimble remembering

calligrapher Berrigan
carved the Iowa rain

IN THE RAGING BALANCE

i.m. Jack Clarke

Energy, the man said, equals
Eternal Delight. Does our return to it
mean shedding all that was our art?
Task of The Living: to ask questions
of The Dead. You did it well, you
Weird and Funny Dude! I thank you
and wish you a good Eternal Night
in Tunisia or wherever you've taken
The Show. "The winds on the moon
blow so cold, so cold" could be a refrain
but isn't nor will this last line rhyme
with anything but tears then again why
should it be the last line and come to
think of it it couldn't possibly be

SEVEN YEARS SHORT OF A HUNDRED

Grandpa was struck at his desk
fountain pen stopped in mid-sentence

It was in his house I discovered
the monumentally baffling Ezra Pound
greenish photo of puffy-faced poet
on glossy black cover   & his better half Dr. Williams

They got me off the old metric train
flew me through dandelions
zoomed me down to a nail in a woman's shoe
up to the top of Niagara Falls   back to a sunset
over Mount Taishan   forward to minuscule mysteries
in undisclosed   wholly interior locations

Later   in London   Pound long gone & forgotten   Eliot
gray eminence glimpsed   slouching towards the elevator

WORDS FOR JOE CARDARELLI (SOME OF WHICH HE HAD HEARD BEFORE)

gone? suddenly
gone? just a moment ago
we stood on a ridge & saw
Earth go into its slow
backflip away from the Sun

sat around Assateague lantern
hissing its core sound to murmurs
on all the "uncertainties, mysteries, doubts"
we loved to roam in   & make our home
in drift & dream   pathos & farce
being poets together   boyishly plausible
even as graybeards

time gone   suddenly gone
but our time was the time that's all *around* the time
we commonly think is all the time there is
smoky lamp-lit globules of time
twenty years   from first days in your town
dear free-bop poet friend   kind wit   big heart

but now a time has come that proclaims
gone   suddenly gone
& leaves us staring at a broken drum

or is it a match   struck   flares in the dark
quark flits through molecule & is gone
to traverse   yet another room

deities' noses twitch in their slumbers
remember poetry & pinball
love   making no demand for love in return
"para siempre" I said yes for ever now
talking   it never was easy to stop
once we got going

WHY THERE IS A CAT CURFEW IN OUR HOUSE

Wake up 5 a.m. to this *yattering* in the kitchen
think: they must've come in through the cat door
switch on light see three teenage raccoons
at the cat food   but now confused
trying to walk through walls complaining louder
not heeding my hoarse "shoo—shoo"

Uh-oh! cat door *flies* open! & with a growl and a snarl
in charges 35 pounds of furious Big Mama Raccoon!
explodes into house   goes straight for bare legs—

startled I slip on the rug fall down the beast keeps on coming
she's getting *larger* I swear she's *inflating* with rage
her young regain courage fan out in attack formation
& do some snarling & growling as well

It is time for reinforcements!
I shout for Jane   she appears in the hall
groggy   stark naked   "what's the matter"
enough to distract this Kali of Procyons

now aware offspring are in good shape
claws scrabbling on floor   she turns
leads fast retreat back into the night

big sighs all around   "hand me the iodine . . . "
so now
we lock the cat door at night
so now you know why
there is a *cat curfew* in our house

& if I were a Victorian poet   there'd be a moral
but late in my century all I can say
is that she did of course remind me of my mother

POUNCES

i.m. Zoaire, 1974-1994

I

one night loud hissing fills the air
it is the venerable Mr. Zoaire
her gato negro lover & familiar
of eighty seasons

fierce flat & frozen to the ground
outside her studio door
he's facing down a band of five raccoons
fanned out & ready to surround & pounce

she saves him from a warrior's death
& now we lock the cat door every night

but we couldn't lock it against the grim reaper

II

small corner of the weave
he slumbered in the sun

III

So, in the great beyond I raise my paw
to strike the lyre sing a praise
of Her who was my life's delight
as I was Hers

(all that much more
in single fading farewell *ping*

& oh, he now says, can't you go on like that?
I really liked the sound of those first lines
but who am I to tell you how to transcribe my ode
you gods have language I don't I
only had a few words when I lived with you
and her
With her, for twenty years
always at home safe wherever she took me
was with me yes talking telling me things
beyond my brain
but not at all beyond my heart
she even taught me to gaze
into her eyes
never a habit of my kind but one I learned
being, if I say so myself, very talented for a cat

IV

here's to you, a toast
a shot of Old Ghost

AND

black walnut foliage   a burst of gold
the cat looks perplexed
the moth it just swallowed
where did it go
the leaves will fall   new ones unfold
the cat won't eat all the moths
friends die before their time
& that is a matter of grief
but she dreams she is swimming
in her studio
her paintings on its walls
make his head swim
into spaces as free of words
as *die Musik*   when it pulls away
into angelic telepathy
shuts up the ape ever scheming
heavy with greed & war
lights him up
so light he becomes
invisible to himself
in a vortex of notes
audible only to the soul
in a world of color and line
where with a sweetly studious air
she's swimming
in her studio's air

A VALENTINE

good to sleep when you're tired
& visit strange cities of the night

& even alone
it is better to wake up
than not to

but it is even better
to wake up next to a loved one

& it is truly amazing
to wake up next to a loved one
& to see the loved one's face
as if you saw it for the first time

"eerily beautiful stranger
asleep in our bed this morning"

o but it's you it's you
I just never saw you this way before

Survival Dancing

In Memoriam Sir Orfeo Joe

The title of this sequence was found on a laundromat bulletin board in upstate New York, in the early summer of 1994:

Survival Dancing
8 P.M., Maplewood Park C.C.
May 12, 19, 26, June 2, 9
Call Bill 273-0126

CANTO ARASTRA

opera creatures   technicolor elves
love to roam in profusion
make home in voices   shouting at no one
dotty shamans   pathos & farce transmitters
many birds singing waters gardens in Spain

        but time's grindstone jaws
        surely crunch graybeards
        & smoky lamplit ore
        in fatal history's central city
        sweep twenty years from day

        end of tube proclaims gone
        lineage guests broken drum virtuosi
        gone from free-bop survival dancing

now patriots of the dark
watch earth go silent movie

no poetry no pinball
no dream no pathos confusion
time was a placid pig
now is a shorter drift

        ride ice hold terror
        endure shadow
        light dim flares underground

faster than bubble life travels
metaphysicks away from the sun

                dark balance   every moment
                all gone   & going   things

IN THE MUSIC COMPOSED BY NUTRITIOUS ALGAE

thought lined up pale winter
white sky
tall smooth car
loaded with motionless wings

staircase time
high speed nail into decades
curious shades of what happened
in small misunderstood group of being
engine loiters in thought

toss coin choose stairs a door with home
black hole of childhood
upholstered in cobblestones
mystery & exactitude of human nostrils

store babbling thought
see shadow body years ago
mumbling wooded mantra
gilded leisure morning

face down on tops of forest
begin to look at colors
they are air

then, mouth, what happens?
how did good very good happen?
question, indeed

KINDLY WATER OTHER LEVEL

two found together   construct regard
place comb in hand   part knot exactly
look out windows   collect words

longing walk
bounces special

speak out strange
once daily

"she went right
clearing fence"

a few
still make sense

sing
awe
in joy's wise space

lie in bed
smell gigantic steamships
hug great-grandmother
wake up at dawn
well rested calm
afloat

a vivid weightless bean

BEGINNING & ENDING WITH LINES FROM CHRISTINA ROSSETTI

strange voices sing among the planets
faint insect talk next door
cartoon mind   cartoon cantos
all the broken drums
La Châtelaine
hushes
her bandogs
& some of us speak weird(ly?)
(no; just weird)
but there is time
all around the time
we think is all the time
there is
your pleasure is my pleasure Earth
between walls of crickets
lips move in fluffed-up night
warm shrubs on slopes
dazzled heart thump rhododendron
grown old yet still so green

AT THIS POINT IN L'HISTOIRE

opaque air
                    ways to live
in a country of shadows
cold iron horse forests

done with hanging loose
jump out of sad speak
wrap bliss in tremulous pebbles

              "& how did the French
              revolution begin?"
              (vertical agitation)

laughs lakes willows lady
nests in dry wind on shore
book open
                    on mirror
"a nice walk with the dog"
fast insect talk next door

FAIR POETRY EATS TREMBLING MATTER

Remote Omar
lyrical bug
or bearded time cloud
our public flits through earth
belovéd yard of Allah

"Your century
or mine?"
My century
My pleasure

"My dear that's dashing! Positively Valhallian!"
—Christina *Plutarch*?
or was it Ted for lunch with Rossetti . . .

all now remain in waters far from kin

remains of enormous gringos
punctuated by The Other

WAS THAT REALLY A SONNET?

"human being"
has government

(thought
you were so tiny

"real thoroughbred infinity"
this, we don't have in life

nevertheless &
thanks to you
I'm me once in a while

living this moment in English

"he tossed his clothes
into the past tense"

presence: really tough job
compared to natural flutter

NOW ON TO GHAZAL GULCH

"When did you last see your criteria?"

"Sometime . . . last winter . . . a minute ago . . . "

Pursue   the saying mind
please train of thought   throw samples

All breathe in some air
but someone needs to till the night

Shows him the miniature city: "Pity, really a pity
. . . possible hole in invention . . . "

Sorry I thought you person
I think I run into them

                    (you look
                    other, stroking
                    her

Tiny figures
from the past
troop by
in porkpie hats

And why not
think of them as
"souls free of the body"

GODS WALKED ANIMALS TALKED

trees in windy room
cicadas *possessed*

tall shadow weeds
          you page the heart
when was "think" first in sound?
walk through mind's middle
                    human or rabbit
waves in tune with head

          eye coneflower
bright burning cells
          glad stomp & squeak
what progress after hawk?

megalith or mound
millions covered with snow
          or the great grease
of the longer than we
                    (in living no t.v.)

best bet out of season
bones of gods
                    posited universe
          wake up
smile in the giddy blue
join in the flash of was

                    brains still on

THE WORD THING

the brilliantly non-objective

appeared within
the century
(a.k.a. Francis Ponge)

(big introductory note
many repeated preludes
& fun with angry young

century of the plunderbund
but book an object still recognized
words in tacit envelope
perpetuate
occasional whiff

trees suddenly active *meme*
in seasons' natural pedantry

method is effortless:
translation of autonomous objects
from adept to zygote
in rhapsodic rises & falls

next click, human language—
quite soon, physical density!
voice of things also includes
steely twinkle in eye

ingenious it is
to have refined ear
ah, ancient ocher in graves

aureous bodement, enigmagist fogbow
century of the plunderbund
nevertheless, satispassion
tmesis & terribilità

SI, SI, e.e.

warm legend, blue shadow:
"green day made gold tree"
light pulls love
in courtly poem
under other
tongue-sky, soul-grid, water, heart

years don't mark snow
nor skeletons' faces

sky train wind, nude moving *so*
words walk road
body, scene
(traverse child tiger light

but desert lives across targets
annuls cities
                    disquieted
leaves'
          memory: fire, war

muscle, take book, describe profile
thought follows
see for instance:
invisible nothing

eye forge battle blade
                                        fall, shadow
                                        ashes, fall

(& yes, they wore great big hats, size extra large

AS LEAVES SWEEP PAST

sister & Joe & Mistah Rilke
gone on "home"
                    small remote fish
on yesterday's pile of ashes

now, more people berserk
difficult demons, shattered dogs

no relief
          from this irony circus
end of tube essayistic
art a dead snakeskin
stuffed with live ants
        (& they return from your past
        grins on their silly mugs

eye meets moment, frame turns
sense looks to say what sense may say

        there, then, it hits:
        "you must change
        your terrible habits"

mocking gaze haunts myth
lyrical bug looks inside
happy to see old cloud
way up in the flying dust

& TIME TROTS BY

sad glad hairy drives
top notch roaring suspense
oh the shaggy years

hero food horny young sentences
hot hero food pronto
pronto   tilted charm never scratchy

(mad hatter at the bar
sometimes a ranting satan
rebuffed by furious foot)

life does it
think of it
enjoy a think of it
among the consequences

drive down Countdown Street
summer sad rearranged
by each day's killing power

beauty death power fear
remember
reside in sky with ears

art
loves
funny details

therefore is
a dreaming
& yes   joy!

elitist
for sure

AT EVENFALL

recall enormous heave of moment
la vie en rose
before some Mallarméan blows it into the *vide* or *abîme*

(but *timing egg in storm*
beats driving car through rock
—Albanian proverb

sun shadow fields cast loose
drum vibes in ground moths flutter
"O Lady Time, summer was great"

but now no house of letters stands
Elizabethanly enjoying given song
paradox knots each graduate

yet she'll stay up to read & write long letters
& on still tree-lined streets attend her musings
do art   eat well   never please wicked money

always treat language like a dangerous toy

Notes

1991

Irina Hollo, the author's sister, was a talented singer, accomplished linguist, translator, and a dear and steadfast friend.

"that five-mile-diameter asteroid" would effectively wipe out life as we know it on this planet.

"father's tongue": in this case, Finnish.

"Dis": Lord of the Greek underworld.

"Ubi sunt": Where are they (now)?

"King Sooper's": Destroyer-size grocery (*not* corner) store.

"The Trouble With Being Born": the title of a book by the great E. M. Cioran.

SOME GREEKS

PALLADAS: Alexandrian, ca. 355–430 CE. When I first saw the poem beginning "where the 3 roads meet" I thought of Stalin, Mao, Dzherzhinsky, etc., but as my friend, poet and feminist critic Lorna Smedman pointed out to me, it also applies to our late-20th-century efforts to overturn idols representing oppressive patriarchal power as it is manifested in *all* walks of life, including the arts.

CALLIMACHUS: of Cyrene, ca. 305–240 BCE. Librarian in Alexandria. Erudite and witty poet, regarded as "difficult"—possibly even "cold and cryptic," as a previous owner/marginalia-jotter found a book of my first translations of Pentti Saarikoski. The Herakleitos addressed in the poem is not the philosopher but Herakleitos of Halikarnassos, author of "The Nightingales," presumably one of the great works lost to posterity.

LUCILIUS lived in Rome around 60 CE and is said to have been a friend of Seneca the Stoic.

LUCIAN of Samosata-by-the-Euphrates, ca. 120–185 CE.

RUFINUS: a native of the island of Samos, ca. 130 CE.

PHILODEMOS: ca. 55 BCE, from Gadara in classical Palestine. Lived in Rome.

BLUE CEILING

"never admit you're rich or asleep": "I have never known a man to admit that he was either rich or asleep" —Patrick O'Brian, *Master and Commander*, p. 177.

"what's ragged should be left ragged": p. 45, Ludwig Wittgenstein, *Culture and Value*.

"mad as Cassandra . . . ": "the wind mad as Cassandra / who was as sane as the lot of 'em" —Ezra Pound, *The Cantos*, p. 475.

"the love that moves . . . ": Dante.

WEST IS LEFT ON THE MAP

Mihail Cosma: author of the poem titled "?" (1927): Romanian poet, b. 1902 in Tirgu-Onca, d. 1968 in Paris. Contributor to the avant-garde journals *75 HP*, *Punct*, *Discontinuité*, and others. From 1928 on, Cosma wrote and published his poetry in French, and also translated Tristan Tzara's Romanian *Primele Poeme* into French. These biographical details, and the poem, gleaned from Manfred Peter Hein's remarkable anthology *Auf der Karte Europas ein Fleck* (A Spot on the Map of Europe; Ammann Verlag, Zurich 1991), a treasury of poems written by poets of the East European avantgarde between 1910 and 1930.

Worstward Ho: Samuel Beckett's prose poem (Grove Press, New York, 1983). Should be recited at every presidential inauguration from now on.

"fights among capos"—capo: (Cosa Nostra) boss.

"Gore, not Peire": "If novels and poems fail to interest the Agora today, by the year 2091 such artifacts will not exist at all except as objects of monkish interest. This is neither a good nor a bad thing. It is simply not a famous thing." (Gore Vidal, in *Screening History*, The New York Times Book Review, 30 August 1992.) For Peire, see Paul Blackburn's wonderful *Proensa: An Anthology of Troubadour Poetry*, University of California Press, 1978.

"watch out / for the wailing Fundees": an ideological mega-gang that seems to be multiplying all over the globe. Its members are particularly keen on killing the *already born*, when and wherever they have reason to suspect that these are championing the cause of rational existence governed by the Golden Rule.

"Odyss   on the old plate": in my late sister's copy of Gustav Schwab's *Die schönsten Sagen des klassischen Altertums* ("The Most Beautiful Tales of Classical Antiquity"), 1925 edition.

"one of those invisible beasties": in the first novel written and published in the Saame (Lapp) language, author Johan Turi speaks of the "invisible animals of Saameland."

"remember Bear's Head": Bear's (or Bear) Head was a Southern Arapaho of the mid-19th century; see pp. 63-66 in: *Chief Left Hand, Southern Arapaho* by Margaret Coel, University of Oklahoma Press, 1981.

"said Ted in a poem": "Today in Ann Arbor (for Jayne Nodland)," in *So Going Around Cities*, Blue Wind Press, Berkeley 1980.

"pulvis et umbra": dust and shade (we are); "il faut s'amuser, non?": one must amuse oneself, no?

"think 'son' / *walking through a geometry*": the lines on the right, which may be read as more or less aleatory "marginalia" *or* heard and seen to resonate with the lines West, come from a page of aphorisms by the Swedish sculptor Ivan Liljander that I picked up in 1992 at a posthumous exhibition of his quietly radiant three-dimensional abstractions at the Thielska Galleriet in Stockholm.

"in Heaven which was the darkest corner": see *Herakleitos and Diogenes*, translated from the Greek by Guy Davenport, Grey Fox Press, 1979.

"Gerry Mulligan play 'Waltzing Matilda'": on *I Giganti del Jazz* #49, 1976.

"caught in the chandelle of our days"—chandelle: abrupt steep climb of airplane propelled by the plane's momentum.

NOT A FORM AT ALL BUT A STATE OF MIND

Epigraph: Hugh Wittemeyer (ed.), William Carlos Williams and James Laughlin: Selected Letters (New York: W. W. Norton, 1989).

(I) "we are but older children . . . ": Lewis Carroll, *To Alice*.

(III) "you know how to walk into a bar": Robert Creeley to the author, one evening in the early seventies.

"amor armor amok emery immure": alternatives to *amore* provided by "Spell Check."

(IV) "it is well known . . . ": from E. S. Bates, *Touring in 1600*.

(V) "landing a B-52 . . . ": Scholar, poet, and musician Jack Clarke describing the task of dying to Ed Sanders, in a telephone conversation not long before Jack's takeoff.

(VI) "the sound like a thousand falling bird beaks / in the brown harpsichord of the grass": Piero Heliczer (*The Soap Opera*, London: Trigram Press, 1967), who also wrote

> i cross the street then immediately cross back again
> i never look to left and right when i cross a street
> why else are street crossings put there if not to cross

—and was hit and killed by a truck around the time of my writing of these fourteen-liners; Piero Heliczer (1937–1993), Italian-born American poet, Personist Surrealist, author of *You Could Hear the Snow Dripping and Falling into the Deer's Mouth*, *The First Battle of the Marne*, and other poetic and cinematic works.

(VII) "days when the giant . . . ": lines from Swedish poet Gunnar Harding's poem "Many Were Here But They Left Again." There are other echoes and near-quotes from that magnificent poem in this humble text, and similar embeddings of lines from Cavalcanti (in translations by Ezra Pound and Marc Cirigliano), Sir Thomas Wyatt, Edwin Denby, Ted Berrigan, Jouni Inkala, and Tom Raworth.

(VIII) "the pneumatic drill destroys my cities": Heliczer, *op.cit.*

(IX) "in the year 1327 . . . ": Francesco Petrarca, Sonnet 211, translated by Nicholas Kilmer.

(X) "at night the streets are tidal like the sea": Heliczer, *op.cit.*

SMALL DOOR AT FAR END

(II) "my poetry . . . " and "they do my . . . ": Ted Berrigan.

(III) "le plus souvent . . . ": Guillaume Apollinaire.

(IV) "it is important . . . ": Ted Berrigan.

LINES FROM TED: AN ARS POETICA

The epigraph, and all the lines of this work, derive from a transcript of two workshops given by Ted Berrigan (1934–1983) in July 1982, at the summer session of the Jack Kerouac School of Disembodied Poetics.

It is, naturally, dedicated to him, and also to the memory of Blaise Cendrars, the author of *Kodak* (and many other great works).

PTERODACTYLS

(I) "*Publication date first of October*": In the summer of 1993, I translated *War Journal* by Zlatko Dizdarevic, the editor of Sarajevo's only surviving newspaper *Oslobodjenje*. The English-language edition of the book was published by Fromm International, New York, in 1994.

convivencia: The period, 711–1492 CE, in which Jews, Muslims, and Christians coexisted in the abundant civilization of al-Andalus in what is now Spain.

"The art of being a slave is to rule one's master": Diogenes.

(IV) This was written in Salt Lake City, Utah (= Deseret, in LDS parlance), in the mid-eighties, thus quite some time before a certain self-styled Serb "poet" began a war of genocide and extermination against Bosnia and specifically its capital, Sarajevo. Tomaz Salamun is the greatest living poet of dead Yugoslavia, and now, mercifully, still-alive Slovenia.

"son, write longer lines": my father told me that, a thousand years ago.

VILLONELLES

Ecologically correct—*re-cycled*, or translated, in large part, from *Or, to Hocus the Animals of the Pursuers by Changing Their Dream Cassettes (old Thibetan Trick)*, first published by Joe Cardarelli's and Kirby and Rosemary Malone's Phantom House Pod Books (Baltimore, 1977).

(VI) "in the world to come . . . power of infinity" paraphrases entries in the notebooks of Novalis (Friedrich von Hardenberg, 1772–1801)

REVIEWING THE TAPE

Ninety-nine per cent of the lines in this text were selected by aleatory numerical methods from my *Sojourner Microcosms: Poems 1959–77.*

HIGH BEAM

HOKA HEY: Aye . . . we were more concise and cheerful than Mr. Tennyson.

PROPOSAL: David Jones (1895–1974), Anglo-Welsh author of *The Anathemata, In Parenthesis*, and other stunning word tapestries; also a painter and world-class calligrapher, creator of exquisite forms of capital lettering suited for carving in stone.

The Berrigan lines are from "Anti-War Poem" in Ted's book *In the Early Morning Rain* (London and New York: Cape Goliard, 1970). Twenty-odd years later, they appear as appropriate as they were then.

A TOWN DEDICATED . . . : title borrowed from a health-food magazine article on Boulder, Colorado, where the author resides.

SCHILLER'S ROTTEN APPLES: Legend has it German *Romantisch* poet Friedrich Schiller (1759–1805) kept rotting apples in his desk drawer and would occasionally sniff them "for inspiration."

"Chet": the one and only.

O KEATS WHERE IS THY STING: "*nell' mezzo cammin*"—Dante: "in the middle of (life's) road."

FROM THE HELLIAD: "bulldog faces of ex-generals"—Andrei Codrescu on National Public Radio, 1991.

QUESTIONS: "Josef Hellström" = Joe Hill.

INHABITED EYES: "falcon-eyed Montcorbier" = François Villon.

WORDS FOR JOE CARDARELLI (SOME OF WHICH HE HAD HEARD BEFORE): "uncertainties, mysteries, doubts" from John Keats's famous 1817 letter: "*Negative Capability*, that is, when man is capable of being in uncertainties, Mysteries, doubts, without any irritable reaching after fact & reason." The poem contains lines from poems written over the years and dedicated to Joe Cardarelli (1944–1994), dear poet, painter, friend.

WHY THERE IS A CAT CURFEW IN OUR HOUSE: Procyon: Greek for "before the dog," name of a star near Orion that rises a little earlier than Sirius (the "Dog Star"), and also the scientific name for the raccoon.

SURVIVAL DANCING

CANTO ARASTRA: "arastra": millstone(s) used to grind up ore; probably from Spanish arar, to till. First noted both word and object on a drive to Central City, Colorado, an old mining town now abandoned to slot machines, with Joe Cardarelli in late April 1994. Four months later, Joe suddenly departed from the human universe. "Survival Dancing" is dedicated to his memory.

BEGINNING & ENDING WITH LINES FROM CHRISTINA ROSSETTI: "La Châtelaine": The mistress of a chateau.

"her bandogs": Dogs kept tied to serve as watchdogs or because of their ferocity.

The medievalism harks back to a dream Paul Blackburn once told me, and to my reading of William Watson's excellent novels *The Knight on the Bridge* and *Beltran in Exile*. And, as we all know, we are presently living in a re-make of the Middle Ages.

AT THIS POINT IN L'HISTOIRE: "& how did the French / revolution begin": Alas, that day (in . . . was it 1946?) I had not memorized the relevant page in my history textbook; all I was able to come up with, under the history teacher's stern gaze, was the first sentence of that descriptive prose: "On the fourteenth of July, all the church bells of Paris began to toll . . . "

FAIR POETRY EATS TREMBLING MATTER: "Remote Omar": Apart from its enjoyable interior resonance, the line refers to Persian poet Omar Khayyám (?–c.1133) who was memorably Englished by Edward Fitzgerald (1809–1883) and later quoted by Ogden Nash (1902–1971) in his lines "I myself am more and more inclined to agree with Omar and Satchel Paige (c. 1906–1982) as I grow older: / Don't try to rewrite what the moving finger has writ, and don't ever look over your shoulder."

"Positively Valhallian": Valhalla was the pleasure dome to which slain Scandinavian warriors were transported from the battlefield by large and fierce angelic females, known as *Valkyries*, for continuous after-hours entertainment until the end of the world (a.k.a. *Ragnarök*).

"Christina *Plutarch*?": Clearly, a brief moment of confusion on the intergalactic internet—possibly even a flashback from a future when Christina Rossetti (1830–1894) and Mestrius Plutarchus (c. 48–c.121), both of them writers on philosophical subjects, may seem practically contemporary. A prolific educational author whose influence extended well into (note!) Medieval times, Plutarch spent the last thirty years of his life as a priest at Delphi. Rossetti was a celibate priestess of the

High Anglican deity, her last work being *The Face of the Deep: A Devotional Commentary on the Apocalypse.*

"or was it Ted for lunch with Rossetti . . . ": The Rossetti of this line could also be Christina's brother, Dante Gabriel (1828-1882), poet, painter and translator, whose turbulent career as a member of the Pre-Raphaelite Brotherhood would seem more compatible with the life and times of New York School member Ted Berrigan, poet of major verbal leaps and bounds both at, and even when out to, lunch. The scribe suspects, however, that it is Christina, to whose sonnets a younger critic has recently compared Ted's work (happily available again in a Penguin *Selected Poems*). Unlike either Christina or Dante Gabriel, Ted liked to refer to friends in his poems by their first names. The scribe regrets any possible confusion arising out of his adoption of this practice; now that you know which Ted is intended, you should hasten to the nearest book emporium and acquire a copy of the *Selected*. It will restore some sanity to your life.

Commentary: The 'author,' who is quite postmodernly used to dwelling inside inverted commas, and prefers the term 'scribe,' is invoking a number of temporal precursors and considering the ways in which their "fair poetry" ("fair" in any sense) ingests their "trembling matter" and possibly survives for a while (until Ragnarök) in some non-corporeal form, while the corporeal ones are transmuted into "bug" or "cloud," and the "public" also "flits through earth." The play on "remain" and "remains" in the last three lines may, tangentially, refer to theoretical and canonical arguments of recent years.

WAS THAT REALLY A SONNET? No names in this one, but three sets of full quotation marks. Most days, it can seem quite hard to utter the term "human being" with a straight face. As for whether it "has government," well, this country presently seems in the clutches of what Ezra Pound describes in Canto LXII (paraphrasing John Adams): "republican jealousy which seeks to cut off all power / from fear of abuses does / quite as much harm as a despotism" (The Cantos, p. 344). "real thoroughbred infinity" is an equally nice but questionable notion, and "he tossed his clothes / into the past tense" is a moment of old-time narrative that may indicate the futility of attempts to describe spontaneous abandon. The two *yous* in the text may be one and the same; the *I* claiming to be *me* "once in a while" probably is. The title is really an afterthought and may be spoken or shouted by the reader.

THE WORD THING: "(a.k.a. Francis Ponge)": 1899–1988, author of *Le parti pris des choses* ("Taking the Side of Things") and many other books of poetic meditation on "word" and "thing."

"century of the plunderbund": *Plunderbund*: a league of commercial, political, or financial interests that exploits the public.

"trees suddenly active *meme*": A *meme* is to your culture as a gene is to your body.

"aureous bodement, enigmagist fogbow": The 'enigmagists' were a loosely knit group of young poets attending the Jack Kerouac School of Disembodied Poetics in 1994–5.

"nevertheless, satispassion / tmesis & terribilità": *Satispassion*—penitential suffering; *tmesis*—the separation of the elements of a compound word by the interposition of another word or words, e.g. "far effin' out"; *terribilità*—effort or expression of powerful will and immense angry force.

SI, SI, e. e.: cummings, who else.

AS LEAVES SWEEP PAST: "art a dead snakeskin": statement attributed to Ingmar Bergman by Swedish critic Leif Zern in his book *Se Bergman* ("See Bergman"), 1993.

"you must change / your terrible habits": paraphrase of Rilke's "You must change your life."

AT EVENFALL: "*la vie en rose*": French pop song the scribe remembers from his childhood, sung by a.o. Edith Piaf and his sister.

"blows it into the *vide* or *abîme*": "void" and "abyss," two words much favored by French Modernist (and even post-Modernist) poets, over American/English "empty" (or e-ness) and "hole."

Rilke's poem "Autumn Day" is echoed in the lines "O Lady Time, summer was great", "stay up to read . . . " and "still tree-lined streets."

"always treat language like a dangerous toy": "Out of the green trees across snow as pure as salt. It is so pure it treats English like a toy." —Edward Dorn, Afterword to *Sojourner Microcosms*, 1977.

COLOPHON

This book was set in Bembo and Shannon Book typefaces. It was printed on acid-free paper, and smyth sewn for durability and reading comfort.